ADVERTISING

K GOWRI | ASSISTANT PROFESSOR | NEHRU ARTS AND SCIENCE COLLEGE | COIMBATORE | TAMIL NADU

Contents

Preface

This book is an introductory roadmap to the advertising process. Advertising is explored as a creative communication message from a brand, created by advertising agencies and distributed across different media to target the right consumers.

The book provides an understanding of the benefits of advertising, and its role in the economy and, even more so, acknowledges that advertisements are not only about selling but also about effectively communicating a message. The creative and conceptual approach toward the communication process is discussed, and insight is presented into the dynamics within the industry and the different stakeholders involved while recognising how different creative elements in advertisements are consciously selected to make them appealing. Finally, it considers how to analyse and measure an advert's effectiveness and looks ahead to future ideas and technologies arising in advertising. Effectively combining theory with practical insight, each chapter begins with learning objectives and ends with key learnings.

Taking students step by step through the advertising process, is important reading for undergraduate and postgraduate students studying Advertising, Brand Management, Marketing Communications and Media Planning.

Prologue

The most important way for businesses to succeed in their activities is to follow their environment carefully and try to integrate innovations into their bodies. In short, businesses must adopt the latest developments to maintain their existence in a fiercely competitive environment. Marketing is one of the business functions that must keep up with these developments. In recent years, significant improvements have been made in the marketing efforts of businesses. They have started to plan their marketing activities within the framework of different perspectives and techniques. In recent years, the concept of value began to take place at the centre of marketing activities.

Today, value is important almost for all businesses. There are different ways of creating value in marketing. In other words, the value that will be offered to consumers as a business can be evaluated in a wide range starting from the presale stages of the product to the after-sale periods. Therefore, the way of creating value can include using technology, empowering employees, etc. However, it is a fact that the basic condition of providing value in marketing is to make strategic marketing planning value-oriented. The digital age and its implications also influenced the firms' marketing activities. The transition to the digital age has made it necessary to make significant changes to many aspects from the design stage of the products to the sales stage and even after-sale services. Consumers of the digital age have started to act consciously and have information about products as well as sales forces. With the introduction of digitalization, physical stores are gradually being replaced by virtual organizations. Electronic commerce has been adopted by many businesses as an effective way of marketing their goods and services.

The transition to the digital age also had an impact on sales management activities. In other words, the presence of the digital environment has both created a variety of challenges for businesses and sales forces and also has facilitated sales forces' activities. Especially in recent years sales forces, who strive to operate in a more value-oriented manner, have further increased their consulting roles. It is understood that the main task of the sales forces is not only to sell but also to provide information on various topics such as product and price comparisons to the consumers. This necessitates more careful selection and orientation of salesforces. It should be also noted that sales visits are now more effective using technological tools. In short, thanks to technological tools, the visual presentation of products is made more effectively than before. This facilitates the persuasion of consumers in the selling stage.

CHAPTER ONE

Introduction to Advertising

Introduction to advertising- History of Advertising- Functions- Significance of Advertising- Key Players in Advertising- Types of Advertisement- Steps in Developing Advertisement

INTRODUCTION TO ADVERTISING

Advertising is a form of communicating information, for persuasive purposes for products (goods, services and ideas) by acknowledged sponsors through numerous media. *Albert Lakert*, also known as the father of advertising, defined advertising as "salesmanship in print, driven by a reason why."

Advertising is directly related to groups of people, rather than to individuals and therefore, it is a non-personal or mass communication. Those individuals could be consumers, people who buy products or business people who would buy large quantities of products for resale in their stores. Mass communication in advertising is very important because the whole purpose of advertising would be to get the message across to those who will purchase goods, to consumers.

Advertising also helps in promoting services and ideas. In terms of the channel of communication, its purpose is to be a medium. An advertising medium is any non-personal means used to present an ad to its target audience. For example, we have radio advertising, television advertising, newspaper ads, and more. Advertising is just one type of marketing communication. Marketing communications are the various efforts and tools used to communicate with customers and prospects, including solicitation letters, newspaper ads, event sponsorship, publicity, telemarketing and many more.

HISTORY OF ADVERTISING

The history of advertising reaches the preindustrial age. The preindustrial age indicates the beginning period of written history and approximately the start of the nineteenth century. Up to the industrial revolution, advertising and production remained primarily a local phenomenon. Items such as land, slaves, and transport (goods and services) were the ones that were promoted. After the invention of paper and Gutenberg's printing press, advertising started to develop and it became more popular. People no longer had to rely on their memories, and they had posters, handbills, and signs to remember them of certain products or services. The Industrializing age, which lasted until the end of World War I, improved advertising with great social and economic changes. Specifically, Industrial Revolution provided the need and means for mass, non-local marketing, which in turn led to mass advertising. People left subsistence farming and moved to the towns and the factories.

Mass printing eventually led to the development of newspapers, which favoured advertising, because now advertisers had more room to put their offers and promotions, which also favoured their business. The industrial age was significant by changing the focus from the production aspect, as indicated in Industrializing age. The industrial age was a period from the end of World War I, until the 1970s. The importance of this period in history lies in the fact that products were branded and promotion was greatly emphasized. Some of the extremely popular products were Coca-Cola, Jell-O, Kellogg's Corn Flakes, and Campbell's soup.

Furthermore, newspapers were not the only source where people could advertise goods and services, advertising became popular on the radio as well. Radio had a great role in promotion because radio stations had specific programs that included advertising so that people could know when to tune in for the program. Television also played an important role, because after World War II, advertising grew rapidly and television reached its position as the largest advertising medium in terms of profits. As time went by and the products became more appealing due to the promotion and the design they had, advertising emphasis shifted from the product features to brand image or personality. For example, Cadillac became the worldwide image of luxury, the consummate symbol of success.

Later, due to the poor economic situation in the world, many turned to more cost-effective sales promotion alternatives, such as coupons and direct marketing. For example, By 1990, advertising had lost 25 percent of its share of the marketing budget to other forms of marketing communications. As technology started to develop and grow, advertising was affected by it, especially with the emergence of the Internet. Today, advertising daily occurrence that surrounds us. It is inevitable and it is everywhere, in every type of media.

OBJECTIVES

- To introduce a new product by creating interest for it among prospective customers.
- To support personal selling programme. To reach people inaccessible to salesmen.
- To enter a new market or attract a new group of customers.
- To fight competition in the market and to increase sales.
- To enhance the goodwill of the enterprise by promising better quality products and services.

FUNCTIONS

Advertising has become an essential marketing activity in the modern era of large-scale production and severe competition in the market.

i) Promotion of Sales:

Advertising promotes the sale of goods and services by informing and persuading people to buy them. A good advertising campaign helps in winning customers and generating revenues.

(ii) Introduction of New Products:

Advertising helps in the introduction of new products in the market. A business enterprise can introduce itself and its products to the public through advertising. Advertising enables quick publicity in the market.

(iii) Support to Production System:

Advertising facilitates large-scale production. The business firm knows that it will be able to sell on a large scale with the help of advertising. Mass production will reduce the cost of production per unit by making possible the economical use of various factors of production.

(iv) Increasing Standard of Living:

Advertising educates people about the products and their uses. It is advertising which has helped people in adopting new ways of life and giving up old habits. I

(v) Public Image:

Advertising builds up the reputation of the advertiser. Advertising enables a business firm to communicate its achievements and its efforts to satisfy the customers' needs to the public. This increases the goodwill and reputation of the firm.

(vi) Support to Media:

Advertising sustains the press. Advertising provides an important source of revenue to the publishers of newspapers and magazines and the producers of T.V. programmers.

SIGNIFICANCE OF ADVERTISING

Advertising helps in spreading information about the advertising firm, its products, qualities and place of availability of its products and so on. It helps to create a non-personal link between the advertiser and the receivers of the message.

The significance of advertising has increased in the modern era of large-scale production and tough competition in the market. Advertising is needed not only for manufacturers and traders but also for customers and society. The benefits of advertising to different parties are discussed in the following paragraphs.

KEY PLAYERS IN ADVERTISING

In the process of advertising, some specific players deliver different functions, the entire combination of which constitutes the entire intricate mechanism of advertising. These five players are:

- **Advertiser**

The advertiser is the company whose product or service is going to be promoted through the incorporation of advertising. In the eventual realm of affairs, the impact of the final advertisement is going to leverage him the most as it's his brand whose future depends upon the nature of the advertising.

- **The advertising agency**

While the advertiser will get affected the most (positively or negatively), it's the advertising agency, which plays the greatest role in generating the impact of the advertisement. In other words, the advertising agency is verily responsible for the magnitude of the effectiveness of the advertisement, the outcome of which will make or break the brand.

- **The Media**

As for the media or the medium that will be chosen to deliver the advertisement, these different media that include electronic, print and interactive media, which constitute the channels of communication that will be employed to enhance the reach factor for the brand. The better and more compatible the media (channel of communication) is, the greater the outcomes of advertising.

- **The Vendors**

Vendors are not directly related to any of the above-mentioned stakeholders. They have an indirect yet significant relationship with the advertising procedure. Consisting of players like freelancers, consultants and self-employed professionals, the vendors provide aegis to the advertiser in helping him and the advertising agency to achieve the optimum quality of advertising that will not only be substantial but would also exude adequate charm.

- **The Audience**

Advertising begins with the advertiser, the person or organization that initiates the advertising process. Advertisers decide the target audience, media, advertising budget and length of the campaign. The advertiser initiates the advertising efforts by identifying a market problem that advertising can solve

TYPES OF ADVERTISEMENT

1. Display Ads:

This is the updated version of newspaper advertising. It's the same concept but in 21st-century form. It means buying ad space on sites that are of interest to your target demographic. You can create text ads, which essentially look just like traditional print media ads, the floating banner above the site's contact and even wallpaper with your product or service on the site background. This is now the most common form of advertising and it's very reasonably priced if you shop around.

2. Social Media Ads:

Pinterest, Instagram, Facebook and pretty much all social media sites offer relatively inexpensive advertising. Paid social media ads are the kind of advertisement that focuses on reaching your target audience with how much you pay adjusted to how many see it and engage with it. Organic social media ads are the kind of advertisement that generates lots of word-of-mouth. Say you post something to your business Facebook page that offers a free product if followers click Like and tag a friend – that is the type of advertisement that is free to post and makes people aware of what you have to offer.

3. Newspapers and Magazines:

These kinds of advertisements are traditional yet no less effective. Combining this type of advertisement between local, statewide and national print media is a great marketing campaign strategy. Plenty of people still reach for their morning newspaper or love to settle down with a hard copy of a magazine. Also, most print media now has a digital presence and can combine these types of advertisements with their virtual version.

4. Outdoor Advertising:

Now that billboards have gone digital it's a huge way to make an effective statement. Transit ads are another kind of advertisement that falls under the outdoors umbrella – feature your product or service on buses, taxis, bike messenger services and pedicabs. Promoting this way gives you excellent brand recognition as these types of advertisements are seen everywhere daily and make your offering hard to forget.

5. Radio and Podcasts:

Verbal promotion is a type of advertisement that can be repeated often as part of radio or podcast shows. You can have a traditional type of ad recorded to be played or there is also the chance of sponsorship. Narrow down the types of podcasts your target audience subscribes to or the station they most listen to for creating the kind of advertisement customers like and remember.

6. Search Engine Marketing:

Search Engine Marketing is curating search engine optimization (SEO) techniques to reach your target audiences more effectively when they search for you. These types of advertisements are Pay Per Click, which means you bid on keywords most associated with your service or products and pay for your results to be at the top of the search engine search. The other one is Cost Per Thousand, which means paying a flat rate to show up in search results 1,000 times.

7. Video Ads:

This type of advertisement engages with your target customers on a digital level. Create a short video and post it on your social media or pay to have it run on sites like YouTube, Hulu and blogs. A video ad can be created by experts from an agency or even done by your in-house team – even if that team is comprised of just yourself.

8. Product Placement:

This kind of advertisement is seen more and more. If you pay for a podcast host to mention using your product or pay a television show to feature a character talking about or using your service, that is product placement. You can also talk to popular YouTube channel hosts about this type of advertisement.

9. Event Marketing:

Paying to sponsor a sports team or a charity benefit falls under event marketing. These types of advertisements mean a large cross-section of people hear your brand name and associate it with that event. Many companies also look to conventions for this sort of niche advertisement.

10. Email Marketing:

A kind of advertisement that is focused on your existing customers, email marketing involves them signing up for promotional sales or newsletters focused on your brand. Email marketing is an updated customer loyalty promotion and works very well when you treat customers as insiders with VIP knowledge.

STEPS IN DEVELOPING ADVERTISEMENT

- **Defining the Product or Service:**

Before developing the plans and strategies for advertising, the product or service offered by the company is clearly defined. This means that the position of the product in the market is determined. You have to understand the product and its customer base to effectively market it to the people at large. It is also important to understand the primary objective of the product or company.

- **Understanding the Target Audience:**

This is an important step in creating a strategy for advertising. Various factors are to be considered for determining the target audience such as demographic factors, psychographic factors, behavioural patterns, etc. The advertising plan is created after considering these factors. E.g. cosmetic and beauty products are aimed at the women's audience.

- **Market Research:**

Once the target market is determined, the next step is to study the market for that particular product. Research about the products already available in the market, what problems are faced in getting those products, what the consumer desire from such products and other issues.

- **Developing a Marketing Plan:**

The strategies formed with the help of market research can be put down as the plan of action for marketing the product. This means, that a marketing plan is created after determining the current trends in the market. The marketing plan aims to create a niche for the product so that it stands out from the competition.

- **Deciding on Communication Media:**

The marketing plan is put into action using various channels of communication. It is important to choose the right media or a media mix for advertising. This depends on the product or service that is being marketed. The choice of the medium is made after considering the target audience and market research.

- **Budget:**

The budget may be determined either before or after creating an advertising strategy. It can be based on the resources available to the company. If the company has an expensive budget, it can carry out high-impact advertising extensively. They can create effective advertising strategies without worrying about finance.

- **Marketing Methods:**

The company can consider two types of methods to advertise while creating the strategy. They are the push method and the pull method. They can decide to go with either depending on their strategy and objective. The push method aims to convince the retailers or salespeople to promote the product, whereas the pull method is directly aimed at the consumers.

- **Modifying Advertising Strategy:**

This process does not end with creating and implementing the advertising strategy. One has to stay in touch with the trends in marketing and modify the marketing strategy from time to time.

CHAPTER TWO

Advertisement Design

Advertisement Design – Appeal-Design-Appeals- Creating Advertising- Types ofAdvertising Appeals-Steps involved in Design and Create an Advertisement - Advertising Effectiveness- Theories of Advertising

ADVERTISEMENT DESIGN

There is neither a magical formula nor pre-defined rules to combine lines, colours, images, typefaces, and other graphic elements to create an eye-catching ad. However, the design depends upon the requirement of the client and the features, functions, appearance, and nature of the product.

Execution of a well-thought-out layout and design has an impressive effect on consumers. A smartly articulated design encourages or in other words subtly compels people to buy the product.

WHAT ARE ADVERTISING APPEALS?

Advertising appeals are communication strategies that marketing and advertising professionals use to grab attention and persuade people to buy or act. In rhetorical theory, the idea of an "appeal" dates back to Aristotle, who identified the three main appeals of communication (also known as the rhetorical triangle): ethos, pathos, and logos, or, in modern language, credibility, emotion, and logic. The idea was that, if you can establish yourself as credible (ethos), for example, you are more likely to persuade people. Likewise, if you tugged on your audience's heartstrings (hit their emotions, pathos) or presented a logical argument (logos), you could persuade people to act. In other words, you (or your communication) appealed to people because you were credible, you affected their emotions, or you made logical sense.

DEFINITION: ADVERTISING APPEAL

Advertising is a form of non-personal communication about a product, service, organization, or idea by an identified sponsor. At the core lies advertising appeal which is used to attract the attention of the consumers, effectively influence their feelings and change their attitude in favour of the advertised product/service. It is the connection that consumers feel with the ad. Creating such an appeal encompasses understanding what the consumers want or need and what excites them. As a basis for advertising messages, several different appeals can be used.

TYPES OF ADVERTISING APPEALS

- **Musical Appeals:**

Music can help to capture the attention of a listener because music is often linked to emotions, experiences, and memories, grabbing the attention of those not previously engaged. The use of musical appeals allows for a connection between the product or service and a catchy jingle or piece of music. As an example, Nationwide Insurance uses the well-known 'Nationwide is on your side jingle as an appeal. And since these musical memories are often stored in the long-term recall areas of the brain, many consumers remember the jingles for extended periods. The selection of music can involve an already familiar tune or can involve the creation of an original composition specifically for the advertisement.

- **Sexual Appeals:**

Sexual appeals provide another method for breaking through ad clutter. Nudity and other sexual approaches are common and are often employed using various methods. By using subliminal techniques, the advertisement attempts to affect a viewer subconsciously. For example, an advertisement may use sexual cues or icons to affect the viewer's subconscious, which is seen in ads where men purchase beer to gain the attention of an attractive female.

- **Humor Appeals:**

Humour is a proven appeal type for grabbing attention and keeping it. When consumers find something humorous, it has value because it causes them to watch, laughs and, most importantly, remember. By capturing the viewer's attention, humour appeals cut through the advertising clutter and allow for enhanced recall and improved moods; consumers who are happy associate the good mood with the product and service. E-Trade's talking baby ad campaign provides an example of this appeal, to attract viewer attention through humour. However, humorous ads can be tricky to design because those that aren't received well result in only the ad being remembered, rather than the product or brand.

- **Fear Appeals:**

Fear appeals are widely used because they simply work. Fear can increase a viewer's interest in an advertisement and can heighten persuasiveness, causing consumers to remember these ads more so than upbeat, warm ads. Fear appeals fit particularly well with certain types of goods and services, particularly those products that can eliminate threats or provide a sense of personal security. For example, fear is often used in insurance company ads, focusing on the consequences of an untimely death. Or, a mouthwash ad can invoke a fear of bad breath.

- **Rational Appeals:**

Rational appeals emphasize facts, details, and product benefits. The goal is moving from product awareness and knowledge to liking, product preference, conviction for the product and, finally, purchase. By transmitting basic product information, a rational appeal provides product knowledge. To promote liking and preference, a rational appeal provides logical reasons as to why a particular brand or service is superior to another.

CREATING AN ADVERTISING

There are, however, a few things to keep in mind before you can design and create an advertisement.

STEPS INVOLVED IN DESIGNING AND CREATING AN ADVERTISEMENT

1. The SWOT Analysis of the Product and the Company:

Before analyzing how to create an advertisement that converts into great results, you should start by performing a thorough analysis of the strengths, weaknesses, opportunities, and threats for both, the company and the product that is to be advertised.

2. Set up your Main objectives:

What is the purpose of your advertising campaign? What are your main objectives? Are your goals feasible or not? You should also perform an analysis of these questions and answer them with the utmost sincerity.

3. Research the Market, the Competition, and your Audience:

It cannot consider ready to make an advertisement without conducting proper research on some important factors your campaign depends on.

4. Identify your Target Audience:

Who is more likely to buy your products or services? Responding to this question is yet another important step in setting up your advertising campaign. Should you want to be successful at designing an appealing advertisement, you need to know to whom you are addressing it.

5. Select your Channels:

Based on demographic research, however, will be able to narrow your search to some specific channels of media distribution suitable for your campaign.

6. Brainstorm for Fresh Ideas:

Take all the information you manage to gather up to this step regarding your products and your targeted audience.

7. The Design Process:

This is the hardest part of the entire advertisement creation process. Everything you did until now, each other previous steps, prepared you for this one.

8. Deliver your Advertisements:

Once the designs are ready to be delivered online, based on your selected delivery channels, you can start your campaign.

DEFINITION OF ADVERTISING EFFECTIVENESS

- **by Rick Suttle:**

Advertising effectiveness pertains to how well a company's advertising accomplishes the intended. Small companies use many different statistics or metrics to measure their advertising effectiveness. These measurements can be used for all types of advertising, including television, radio, direct mail, Internet and even billboard advertising. A company's advertising effectiveness usually increases over time with many messages or exposures. But certain advertising objectives can be realized almost immediately.

- **Reach:**

One metric for advertising effectiveness is reached. This measurement pertains to the number of people who saw a company's advertising. Small business owners usually know how many people can potentially see their ads. Local television stations report the number of viewers for certain shows. Similarly, magazines report circulation figures. But not all of these viewers or readers notice the ads.

- **Sales and Profits:**

The best way to build sales and profits is by reaching the right target audience. In other words, small business owners must make sure their advertising reaches the people who are most likely to purchase their products. Companies often develop customer profiles from warranty cards or marketing research to gather this information. Target audience variables or demographics can include age, gender, income and education. For example, a high-end women's clothing retailer may effectively drive sales and profits by targeting women with higher incomes.

- **Brand Awareness:**

Brand awareness is another metric of advertising effectiveness. Brand awareness is the percentage of people who recognize a company's brand of products. Television and radio are two of the best mediums for building brand awareness. Small companies can also build their brand awareness on the Internet by advertising on online Yellow Pages or promoting their wares through major search engines like Google and Yahoo.

- **Testing Advertising Effectiveness:**

Small companies can test their advertising effectiveness in several different ways. One way is to insert certain "word flags" into the advertising messages, according to "Entrepreneur." This may be a simple phrase or word that customers recognize and can, therefore, mention when inquiring about an advertisement. The word flag can also be in the form of a question.

THEORIES OF ADVERTISING

There are 5 Advertising theories explained

1) The Mediation of Reality:

Ads are effective when steered with other media and settings in which they are entrenched. What makes the ads persuasive is how they utilize the media to elicit a world of fiction and that of actions together and not necessarily the content. What the media do in regards to advertising is describe the excitement and addiction by extending and heightening our neural responses.

2) Shifting Loyalties:

Ads know how to play upon and replicate clashed loyalties that keep on changing. Mainly, the ads always try to cultivate a strong sense of loyalty to an individual brand, but they also have a way of urging consumers to alter their loyalties and make an attempt to a rather new thing and primarily renounce old loyalty for a relatively new brand in the market.

3) The Magic of Meaning:

This explains how ads are used in infusing the meaning of the products to the users in addition to selling. It shows how advertisements influence the values and other fundamental beliefs of consumers. It essentially describes how and why ads have gone beyond the frontier of selling products and services and are increasingly becoming involved with the shaping of individual and social values.

4) The Hidden Message:

Ads are used in manipulating and unconsciously misleading the public. Psychologists argue that advertising is treacherous since it uses psychology to create hidden messages that are emotionally loaded. What happens is that since the message is hidden, there is a tendency for viewers' critical resistance to be deluded and reduced.

5) Imitative Desire:

Ads have a way of playing upon consumers' tendency to want what other people also wish. Many theorists have always argued that it is human nature to desire of becoming what other people are especially when the other person is powerful, good-looking or famous. But the truth of the matter is that it's hard to become another person, and it is this castle in the air that keeps the desire alive.

CHAPTER THREE

Media Planning

Media Planning- Indoor –Outdoor-Advertising-Types-Merits and Demerits-Factors Consider Outdoor Advertising

MEDIA PLANNING

Media planning is the process of identifying and selecting media outlets – mainly newspapers, magazines, websites, TV and radio stations, and outdoor placement – in which to place paid advertisements. The person responsible for evaluating the many media options and strategizing campaigns to support a particular product, service, or brand is called a media planner. Media planners typically are employed by advertising agencies.

A media planner's job is to develop a coordinated plan for a particular client's advertising budget. They decide where, when, and how often to feature a specific ad. The more the planner can optimize meaning stretch a client's budget to reach the largest number of people, the better his or her odds of seeing results. The whole purpose of advertising is to make potential customers aware of a company's products or services and to persuade them to buy them.

CREATING A MEDIA PLAN

The goal when creating a media plan is to reach target customers - those who are most likely to buy from you, at the exact moment that they have decided to buy. Using advertising, you can educate and inform those likely customers, to make them aware of your business and persuade them to buy a particular product from you rather than another business

To make that happen as efficiently and cost-effectively as possible, it is important to weigh the following when developing your media plan:

- **Reach:**

One of the two most important factors to consider, reach is the number of people you want to get in front of during a particular timeframe, such as a week or a month.

- **Frequency:**

The second most important factor is frequency, which is the number of times your target customers will see your ad. Obviously, the higher the number, the better, but the cost is also a factor. For example, you may want to run an ad daily in your local newspaper, but the cost for such a purchase may exceed your annual budget.

- **Cost-Per-Thousand:**

One way to measure the cost of advertising is to divide the total cost of advertising in a particular outlet by the media's thousands of customers, to get the cost-per-thousand value. For newspapers and magazines, you'd divide the cost by total subscribers. For blogs, you'd divide by subscribers.

- **Selectivity:**

Depending on how targeted your product is, you may want a measure of how well the media outlet reaches your particular prospect. For example, advertising Rolls Royces through the local newspaper will attract attention, but what percent of the newspaper's subscribers fall into the target market of prospects likely to buy? It might be too low a number to make sense.

- **Impact:**

How many senses can the media outlet be considered to reach? Magazines can appeal to sight, and perhaps smell (with those perfume inserts), while websites can appeal to sight and sound. The same is true with TV. You should consider what senses will make the biggest impact on a customer's purchase decision.

INDOOR ADVERTISING

Indoor advertising represents your messages or services in enclosed spaces such as supermarkets, cafes, restrooms, bus stations, sports clubs, schools and others. It creates an atmosphere in which visitors can easily identify your products and brand. Impress can submit your interior advertising in various forms:

Branding offices stand for exhibitions, restaurants and shops, canvas print, textile posters and others.

TYPES OF INDOOR ADVERTISING

1. Press Media:

Advertisements in newspapers, magazines, journals etc., can be called press advertising. It is the most popular and widely used means of advertising. It is the most economical media of advertisement. The growth of literacy and development of the press also pave the way for these press media.

A. Newspapers:

There is no doubt that newspapers are the best and most popular medium for advertising. It reaches every nook and comer of the country. It is the most powerful selling force. In India, there are many languages. Newspapers are being published in 91 languages. According to statistics, the "Indian Express" daily newspaper is published in 10 places and prints 5,67,801 copies, "When the literacy rate is increasing, this medium can easily be adopted for good results through advertising.

Merits of Newspaper:

- Newspapers are having a large demand and wide coverage.
- The cost of a newspaper is less when compared to its use.
- Wide publicity is possible.
- It contains interesting matters for everybody.
- Speedy preparation and publication of advertising are possible.
- Newspapers are read daily and hence continuous publicity is possible.
- It makes quick results. The public response is quick.
- Regular and frequent advertisement is possible.
- It is flexible i.e., the number of pages and shape of the advertisement can also be changed.
- It is suitable for direct and indirect selling.
- Lengthy matter for advertisement can be given.
- In local newspapers, preference is given to the advertisement of local products.
- Effectiveness of advertisement can be estimated.
- Selection of the market is possible.
- It is news apart from timely.

Demerits:

- It is having the shortest life. "Today's newspaper is tomorrow's waste paper."
- Frequent advertisement is required lest it should become ineffective.

- Newspaper advertising is affected by the illiteracy of the public. Chances for display and demonstration are much rare.
- People read newspapers in a hurry.

B. Magazines and Journals:

These are periodically published. They are published weekly, fortnightly or monthly. Magazines are read leisurely. Magazines are published according to the tastes or liking of the public.

There are different types of magazines:

(a) General Magazines:

General magazines are read in easy chairs. There is generally a lengthy advertisement. The standard of reproduction is also in better way. They give more interesting and longer duration, e.g., Illustrated Weekly, Blitz etc.

(b) Specialists Magazines:

They are technical journals and professional journals. Technicians read technical journals. Doctors, lawyers, accountants etc., read professional journals. There are special magazines for industry, banking, politics, religion, agriculture, insurance, transport, literature etc. Special magazines for women and children are also available.

(c) Special Issues:

Dipawali Malar, Directory (Telephone Directory) are also published which contain a large number of advertisements along with articles, stories, special features etc. Some magazines enjoy national and international circulations.

C. Radio:

Radio is the quickest medium of advertising when compared to newspapers or magazines. Sound moves faster than other media. It is a popular medium of advertising for a commercial firm. Radio makes its appeal to the car. Commercial radio broadcasting has become popular and is widely used in all countries.

It is also popular in India and the radio has started playing an important role as one of the media of advertising. It plays its role well, especially in rural areas where newspapers cannot reach. The maximum number of radio sets is in Tamil Nadu, followed by Maharashtra, West Bengal, and Gujarat. Further, transistorized radio brightens the scope of advertising.

OUTDOOR ADVERTISING

Outdoor advertising passes the message to those people who are moving the audience. Generally, almost all the people go out on some purpose or other-office, walk, sightseeing, journey, park visit etc. This outdoor advertising has the best effects of advertising. Before discussing the types of outdoor advertising, let us discuss the merits and demerits of this advertising.

Merits:

- This is the best for local advertising; it has the widest appeal.
- 2 It speaks to everyone.
- It engages a few seconds of people's time and needs no effort.
- It always attracts the viewers, because of its style and colourful appearance.
- Its effect is permanent.
- It indirectly beautifies the place.
- It is flexible
- It is a low-cost medium.

Demerits:

1. It has fewer advantages, compared to other media.
2. It reduces its value because of brevity.
3. The effect of prospects cannot be measured.
4. It can be used only as a supplementary type of advertising.

TYPES OF OUTDOOR ADVERTISING:

1. Mural Advertising (Posters):

At present this is a common form of advertising. The posters are made in attractive colours in brief and printed. The poster is a sheet of paper. The matter is depicted on it. Then the prepared posters are pasted on walls or boards. Film showers use this medium for advertising and the posters are pasted in such a manner that they are projected to the people at the bus stand, railway stations, marketplace, parks, libraries, and crowded areas.

2. Advertising Boards:

These are also posters, but have better status than ordinary posters. The boards are fixed at the areas where people frequently assemble. Such boards are fixed in decent and neat places. They appear more attractive than posters.

3. Vehicular Advertising:

This moving advertisement finds a place on vehicles-buses, trains etc. The vehicle passes through many places and many people happen to see it.

4. Painted Display:

It is an artist's work. This display is large. It is visible from a distance. It finds a place at crossings, compound walls or erected structures built of poles or pillars.

5. Travelling Display:

These are the advertisements as posters, small in size, written beautifully and placed inside trains, buses, tramcars, vans etc. The travelling people, in these vehicles, repeatedly notice it and keep it in their memory.

6. Electric Display:

The electric display is more attractive. It is popular nowadays. The beauty and attractiveness depend upon the skill of electrical engineers. Another method is that of running bulbs strap and it looks like moving. Such arrangements are common in big cities. During nighttime or in the dark background, it is more bright and alluring. It is costly.

7. Sky Advertising:

Sky advertising and skywriting have become popular. Big balloons with a message written on them or attached to them are allowed to float in the air. Big kites containing advertisements may be floated in the open air. Skywriting is a kind of advertising played by the pilot, through the aeroplane, either by forming smoke or by illumination.

8. Sandwich-Men:

Sandwich men are hired by advertisers. They move or walk down busy roads and streets. They dress peculiarly in fancy clothes. They carry posters of the product of the advertisers. They utter slogans. They create a certain type of musical sound. This sort of advertisement has a short life but is effective. Cinema theatres usually adopt this method of publicity.

9. Handbills (Leaflets):

Handbills are common and too cheap. Handbills, which are in the form of leaflets are distributed among the people through hired men. Sometimes, music bands are also played along with the distribution of leaflets. Only interested persons may go through the handbills. The handbill distributor distributes copies of the handbill to all, who pass nearby. An uninterested person receives it with one hand and throws it away with the other hand. This type of advertising is suitable for small business people.

FACTORS CONSIDER IN OUTDOOR ADVERTISING

There are a few factors determining whether an outdoor advertisement will be successful or not, and they are incredibly important for professional outdoor advertising companies to understand.

Here are a few factors you must consider:

1. Plan a Budget:

Budget is the base of all your advertising plans, it can range from small to very large and is dependent on the type of marketing you want for your product. Making a proper budget plan for the advertisement helps you select the right media and locations you will be using for your outdoor advertisement.

2. Know the Target Market:

Identify your target consumer and start advertising from there. For example, if you are selling clothing for working women, start from those areas which have most of the offices in the city. Outdoor advertising companies will advise their clients about the geographical facts that can decide a successful marketing campaign. Advertising a product on a very large scale yet still unable to find increasing demand in the consumer market? This is usually the result of neglecting to analyze where your target market is and missing the opportunity to best communicate your message to the targeted, potential consumer.

3. Collect Information about your Competitor's Strategies:

Find out who your competition is, and who's already advertising a similar product or service that may have the same appearance as your brand. Then research and analyze them to get useful information. What outdoor advertising strategies are they using? What kind of messages are they conveying? Are these messages precise or are they suggestive? What types of illustrations and visuals are being used? Understanding your competitors will help you boost the effectiveness of your outdoor advertising campaign.

4. Consider Offering Promotional Incentives:

Offers that announce discounts or prizes can be likely to get more attention. Examples include offering prizes for the first few customers, discounts for repeat customers, or cash-based referrals for referring a friend or neighbour. Always be cautious when using this technique though as not to "cheapen" your brand.

CHAPTER FOUR

Broadcast Media

Broadcast Media- Types of Information are Available in the Broadcasting Media- Radio as a Medium- Television as a Medium- Television as a Medium- Internet Advertising- Email Advertising

BROADCAST MEDIA

The term 'broadcast media' covers a wide spectrum of different communication methods such as television, radio, newspapers, magazines and any other materials supplied by the media and press.

TYPES OF INFORMATION ARE AVAILABLE IN THE BROADCASTING MEDIA

The broadcasting media provides valuable information, for example, speeches, documentaries, interviews, advertisements, daily news, financial markets and much more. The latest (newest/most up-to-date) information can be found here.

WHERE CAN FIND IT?

Transcripts (hard copies) of interviews, speeches, programmes, etc., are often available from the supplier of the information, e.g. SABC, M-Net, the specific radio station, etc. Nowadays many of these transcripts etc., are made available on the Internet. The following are just a few links, there are many more:

Broadcast television, Cable television, On-demand television, TV/web integration, Local, network, and national radio, On-air endorsements, Long-form programming, and Multi-language programming.

- **Radio as a Medium:**

Radio reaches more Americans than any other advertising medium. As an example, let's look at Los Angeles, CA. It is the radio revenue market in the world and generates more than 1 billion dollars in sales each year. In that market alone, more than 9 million people listen to the radio each week. People are loyal to the radio and love listening to their favourite DJ or talk show host. The shows become part of their routines as they drive to and from work or run errands or take kids to school. There is probably at least one conversation in your office every day that starts with, "I heard on the radio this morning..." The reason? More adults in L.A. listen to the radio in a week than will visit Google+ in a month!

Radio offers a unique method to achieve Top-Of-Mind-Awareness (TOMA). As people listen to radio advertising and don't rely on visual cues they would get from TV or a website, your ad is playing in a "theatre of the mind". For example, the phrase "a soft pillow" could conjure an image of a white silk pillowcase on a down pillow for one person whereas another person could be thinking of the cute yellow pillow they had as a child. That openness to interpretation means the quality of your copywriting is vital to success. You have an opportunity to connect with a listener through their own experiences, ideas, and dreams.

- **Television as a Medium:**

We just mentioned the unique power of radio to achieve TOMA. Television advertising -another part of broadcast media- is the most powerful medium currently available to put your brand at the forefront of your customer's minds. The combination of audio and visual messages allows for the dual delivery of your marketing message.

- **Television Advertising Choices:**

There is a huge range of choices when it comes to demographic targeting with television advertising. The most basic is network vs. cable. Attach your brand to the prestige and authority of companies such as ABC, CBS, NBC, or Fox. Take advantage of the huge variety of cable networks that enable you to selectively target viewers based on income, hobbies, ethnicity, favourite sports, gender, sexual orientation, education level, or any combination you may need.

Much has been said about the impact of TiVO/DVR devices and people skipping commercials. Multiple studies have shown that advertising on TV continues to be one of the most effective marketing methods available. Only about 50% of DVR-owning households skip commercials. And many of those that skip have been shown to retain what they see in fast-forward or -most importantly- see something that catches their attention and will go back to watch the full ad.

How Do Radio and TV Help My Company?
Credibility via popular media
Branding to a loyal audience
Association with customer's favourite show/actor/DJ/host
Top of Mind Awareness (TOMA)
Unique demographic targeting
Multi-screen engagement

- **Internet Advertising:**

Online advertising, also called online marketing or Internet advertising or web advertising, is a form of marketing and advertising which uses the Internet to deliver promotional marketing messages to consumers. Consumers view online advertising as an unwanted distraction with few benefits and have increasingly turned to ad blocking for a variety of reasons.

It includes email marketing, search engine marketing (SEM), social media marketing, many types of display advertising (including web banner advertising), and mobile advertising. Like other advertising media, online advertising frequently involves both a publisher, who integrates advertisements into its online content and an advertiser, who provides the advertisements to be displayed on the publisher's content. Other potential participants include advertising agencies who help generate and place the ad copy, an ad server which technologically delivers the ad and tracks statistics and advertising affiliates that do independent promotional work for the advertiser.

- **Email Advertising:**

The first widely publicized example of online advertising was conducted via electronic mail. On 3 May 1978, a marketer from DEC (Digital Equipment Corporation).

The first known large-scale non-commercial spam message was sent on 18 January 1994 by an Andrews University system administrator, by cross-posting a religious message to all USENET newsgroups. In January 1994 Mark Eberra started the first email marketing company for opt-in email lists under the domain Insideconnect.com. He also started the Direct Email Marketing Association to help stop unwanted emails and prevent spam.

Four months later, Laurence Canter and Martha Siegel, partners in a law firm, broadly promoted their legal services in a USENET posting titled "Green Card Lottery – Final One?"[15] Canter and Siegel's Green Card USENET spam raised the profile of online advertising, stimulating widespread interest in advertising via both Usenet and traditional email. More recently, spam has evolved into a more industrial operation, where spammers use armies of virus-infected computers (botnets) to send spam remotely.

CHAPTER FIVE

Public Relations

Public Relations- Difference Between PR and Advertising- The effect on the public- Pros & Cons of Advertising- Effects of Advertisements on Society - Influence of Advertisement on Consumers- Drastic Change of Today's Advertisement

PUBLIC RELATIONS

The local news broadcasts a segment on the availability of music, games and internet options via a new cell phone service or a national magazine and covers a story about the amazing new cancer drug being developed by a biotech company-these stories are the results of successful public relations (PR) campaigns. These campaigns most likely included writing press releases, contacting the media, and creating a buzz about the client to entice the media to report on it. While the advertisements produced by ad agencies are easily recognizable, the work of PR firms is much less conspicuous. Public relations, as the title implies, is about managing the public's perception of clients. PR firms work for politicians, entertainers and sports teams as well as corporations.

In addition to trying to get their clients noticed by the media, PR firms also keep track of how and how often their client companies are mentioned in the press. They comb through various publications and other media, clipping articles and compiling the information. PR firms are also called into action when there is a crisis that requires a client to take a public stance. For example, in the case of product tampering decisions need to be made about pulling products from the shelves, assisting victims and their families, and strategies for buoying consumer confidence in the company and its products. A public relations firm will assist their clients in good times and bad to manage their public image.

DIFFERENCE BETWEEN PR AND ADVERTISING

Just like advertising, PR often helps increase sales as well and may include elements of marketing. However, it is mainly focused on creating positive publicity about a particular company, organisation or individual and maintaining a good reputation in the public. By doing so, PR helps create a relationship between let's say a commercial company and its customers who are more likely to choose the products from a company they have a good opinion of over those from a firm they have never heard of before or heard something negative about it.

THE EFFECT ON THE PUBLIC

The public reacts very differently to an add then to a newspaper article or a TV report. They know very well when they are reading/looking at an add and the information they are communicating is perceived with a certain degree of scepticism. They know that the add wants to persuade them to buy a particular product or service and will either believe or disbelieve the information they are communicating. But when they are communicated news about a new product or service through a third party, for example, a newspaper or online article they perceive it as informative and worthy of their attention. A press release for instance does not directly encourage them to buy but it often achieves just that by creating a positive image about the product/service or its manufacturer, or both.

- **Cost:**

Neither a professionally led marketing or PR campaign is inexpensive. The cost depends greatly on who you hire but generally, PR is a lot less expensive than advertising. But it is also true that PR has a lot less control over the way their clients are presented by the media in comparison to paid adds that oblige the media to publish them unchanged.

At the same time, a press release is published only once by a single media, while the ads can be published over and over again.

THE PROS OF ADVERTISING

1. it's an Easy way to Create a Value Proposition:

Prospects need to see that something can solve a problem for them for them to consider making a purchase. Value is often seen as saving someone time or saving them money. Advertising is an easy way to prove that there is a value proposition to be considered with a brand or product.

2. It creates a Way to Set Brands and Products Apart from the Competition:

People today don't just want to buy something that is "good enough." They want to purchase the best product at the best price.

3. It Reaches Multiple Demographics Simultaneously:

Advertising is one of the easiest ways to reach out to multiple target groups at the same time. This action helps a business to better discover who their primary customers tend to be, and the demographics to which they belong and provides information that allows for prospect cloning

4. One Single Target Demographic can also be Emphasized:

Advertising also allows for a business to specifically target one demographic. This is seen every day with direct mail campaigns, email marketing, and even food commercials that air right when people get done with their 9-5 grind and don't feel like cooking. If a business knows when and where it can reach specific prospects, then advertising creates a natural relationship-building point that can help prospects engage because they appreciate the value proposition that has been created.

5. Ultra-Specific Demographics can be Targeted Today:

In the past, advertising was about choosing a certain time of day, a specific zip code, or households that earned a certain amount of money. Today all of these can become filters for an ultra-specific advertising campaign that happens online. This allows a business to find its best customers in the best places and keep replicating those results over a potentially infinite period.

6. It provides Consumers with Information about the Choice:

Every consumer has different personal preferences that make certain products more appealing than others. From flavours to prices to specific product comparisons to show how one product is better, companies can provide information about broad options that can appeal to broad demographics so that consumers can practice their right to choose what products are best for them.

7. Advertising Provides Economic Growth and Support:

When advertising is available in major markets, there is a direct correlation between that market's GDP increase to the amount of advertising that is consumed. This is even true on an industry level within an overall economy. Certain industries that advertise more often have better growth results than industries that don't advertise. Growth is always the liveliest when advertising is a major point of emphasis.

8. Advertising Creates Jobs:

In the United States alone, advertising provides over 18 million jobs that contribute to the economy in various ways. It isn't just in the creative industry either. Improved revenues because of advertising contributes to job growth within the business or industry and this provides more profitability, which eventually leads to more job growth.

9. Advertising Supports a Global Culture:

Without advertising, many of the things we enjoy today would be either more expensive or wouldn't exist at all. All of those costs were covered through advertising sponsorships and incoming revenues from ticket sales and other consumer purchases. The same is true of TV sports broadcasts, art exhibitions, and even grassroots crowdfunding efforts.

10. It's One of the Easiest Ways to Prove Niche Expertise:

One of the hottest forms of advertising that are happening today is the whitepaper, ebook, or article that is allowed to be downloaded for free. This information creates evidence in the minds of B2B and B2C prospects that proves a business has the expertise that can create value.

11. Social and Moral Issues can be Promoted with Ease:

Public advertising campaigns can help to bring more awareness to certain societal issues, such as bullying or homelessness, that may not otherwise be obtained through other sources. These public campaigns may have a cost them from a production standpoint, but because they spur local actions and support, the value comes back around over time and everyone benefits from it.

12. It inspires People:

Advertising can stir the human soul and imagination to create real inspiration that benefits the world. The "God made a farmer" advertisement from Dodge, featuring Paul Harvey, is a classic example of this. Aired during the 2013 Super Bowl, it was 2 minutes of inspiration for America's Heartland that still has people talking.

THE CONS OF ADVERTISING

1. It Costs Time and Money:

Advertising doesn't come cheap. It will always cost time, money, or both to complete successfully. It may not cost someone anything to create a video, but they'll be spending time editing the content of it, using resources to upload it and spending time responding to comments about it.

2. Messages Get Lost in the White Noise of Information Overload:

People today spend less than 5 seconds analyzing data to determine if it is worthy of consumption. If it passes the test, then it will be consumed. If not, then it will simply blend in with the rest of the white noise that occurs on the internet every day. It is very easy for an advertising message to get lost because it doesn't properly communicate value.

3. Results are Never Guaranteed:

A business can spend $1 million on advertising and get $0 in return. The results of an advertising campaign are never guaranteed. This is why so much research goes into demographic research so that problems can be identified and solved by the products that a brand represents.

4. There are a Ridiculous Amount of Platforms that Concept Advertising:

Which platform a targeted demographic prefers to receive their advertising on can be just as costly and time-consuming as the creation of the advertising campaign itself. From billboards to radio, and TV to the internet, there are hundreds of ways that a business could spend its advertising budget.

5. It is Difficult to Stay Unique in Today's Information-Sharing World:

Because an advertising campaign can go global in a matter of minutes [or even seconds] on the modern internet, it is very difficult for a business to be able to stay unique. Successful advertising campaigns can be copied by others so that the successes can be replicated. This requires a business to continually innovate, create, and find new approaches to provide a unique message.

6. Advertising is Often Associated with Media:

Advertising is how most people today receive their media, even if that is from an online source. Two out of three internet users say that there are willing to be exposed to higher levels of advertising just so they can receive more information that can be freely consumed. This still happens in the print world as well since advertising reduces the subscription prices of newspapers or magazines by 50% or more.

7. It is Very Easy for the Wrong Message to be Consumed:

Budweiser discovered this disadvantage of advertising in April 2015 during the next phase of their Up For Whatever ongoing campaign. A slogan was printed on the label of Bud Light bottles that said "The perfect beer for removing 'no' from your vocabulary for the night." The intent was to have people be "up for whatever," like table tennis with Arnold Schwarzenegger or playing real-life Pac-Man. The problem was that many consumers saw this message as promoting rape culture and the backlash against the slogan caused negative publicity for Budweiser instead of a positive campaign.

8. Advertising Always Impacts Someone in Some Way:

Every advertisement that someone views will have either a positive or negative impact on them. Those impacts might be slight, but they could be very large impacts as well. Imagine a recovering alcoholic being exposed to several commercials for beer, wine, and spirits or kids being exposed to product commercials for 5 minutes straight during their favourite cartoon both instances happen with regularity. Because there is no way to control how advertising impacts people on the individual level, businesses are forced to hope that the positives outweigh the negatives.

9. It's a General Nuisance:

Excessive advertising might have a positive effect on the economy, but it tends to hurt consumers when the same type of advertising happens over and over again. This is especially true during election cycles when political advertising takes over the landscape. Hundreds of millions of dollars in advertising may be spent on a single election, exposing people to competing messages that get repetitive and irritating when they are seen several times per hour.

10. The Intended Targets of the Advertising Campaign may Never See it:

The goal of advertising is to reach a specific demographic at a specific time. The only problem is that even with comprehensive research guiding the way, viewing hours are subject to change at any given time. Someone might decide they've had enough of the internet and don't log into social networking sites for a month. A flat tire keeps someone away from the TV at the targeted time they'd normally be watching it. A desired moment of silence causes someone to turn their radio off. Everything can be done correctly, but "fate" can still intervene and create a missed message.

11. Product Placements can Ruin Personal Enjoyment:

Some iconic brand placements have happened over the years. Remember Superman crashing through the giant Coca-Cola billboard? Some ridiculous product placements have ruined experiences for people. Remember the gourmet food enjoyed in Demolition Man at Taco Bell? Product placement could be a $50 billion industry in 2015 and helps to fund entertainment options, but it can be sometimes too aggressive and create a negative effect.

12. It isn't Always Ethical:

Kids under the age of 8 are susceptible to believing everything they see on TV. If a product says it is the best created, kids are going to believe it. If someone is hungry and sees a picture of the pizza, burgers, or unhealthy food options that they are craving, then they'll often decide on unhealthy food instead of making something healthier at home. By its nature, advertising isn't always ethical because it is attempting to influence purchasing decisions so that people spend money they weren't intending to spend.

EFFECTS OF ADVERTISEMENTS ON SOCIETY -

Advertising is a form of communication for marketing and is used to encourage or persuade an audience to continue or take some new action. It is also to show the existence of an organization, providing information about a particular subject that the advertiser needs to inform in form of verbal or technological form. It has a great impact on the producers, consumers and society and now it looks like it has become a necessity for the producers to advertise their product or service in any the means such as television advertising, infomercials, radio jingles, online advertising, press advertising, billboard advertising and so on.

A. POSITIVE IMPACT

1. Growth in Business - The impact of the advertising company on society at large has been enormous. Unprecedented sales have been made the world over by listing products and services on TV. Indian society belongs to the Television age that loves to just sit and watch all sorts of things on television. Research has shown that immense profit has been recorded by most companies who have invested hugely in advertising.

2. Public Service Ads. - Public service advertisements are often the first things considered when people discuss the positives of advertisements. These advertisements market a social concept of importance to the general public. Many public service announcements run messages about health, safety, national security, etc. For example, Amitabh Bachan requests and informs people about polio drops or a common man scared to go to a doctor because of shyness regarding the disease or problem he has.

3. Public being Informed - Needs of the public increase with time. They need more and more products and each time a new one. At the same time, many new products come into the market. Ads. are the mode of communication which keeps the public informed about new things.

B. NEGATIVE IMPACT

1. Extravagance - Ads show the selling price of the commodities. Here we would see that people are tempted by these Ads to buy the goods they cannot afford. Here viewers become extravagant and do not hesitate to use corrupt means to earn more to increase their purchasing power.

2. Controlling Consumer Decision - Consumers have never taken a step back to examine the effects of advertising on their spending habits. Sometimes an advertisement is so good that the average consumer will go out and buy that product only to find out later that what they saw in the advertisement is very different in reality. Today's advertisements use tactics that are invasive and controlling.

3. Vulgarity - Ads Portray Vulgarity also. They exploit the emotions and sentiments of people. They may prove to be offensive to public decency and insult women. Even it may take children on a different path, affecting them negatively.

4. High Prices and Creation of Monopoly - Advertising increases the prices of products to consumers because the expense incurred in it is passed on to the consumers. moreover, the higher spending power of the larger firms as compared to smaller firms may lead to the creation of a monopoly which may be consequently used to exploit customer

INFLUENCE OF ADVERTISEMENTS ON CONSUMERS

- One of the hallmarks of modern capitalism, advertising helps fuel the economy by motivating buyers and supporting sellers. It is typically used in conjunction with other promotional tools, like personal selling, sales promotion and public relations, and is at the heart of marketing strategy for most consumer goods. Advertising influences people through education, persuasion and reassurance.
- **Education:**

Advertising is an effective means of communicating information about products and services to a large number of consumers at once. This information plays a key role in educating people about different brands' functions and features, like how they work, what they cost and where they can be purchased. Because the information in ads comes directly from the manufacturer, it is more likely than secondhand reports to be verifiable and reliable. This helps buyers make choices most likely to satisfy their needs and wants.

- **Persuasion:**

Using creative techniques like direct brand comparisons, advertising can persuade people that one product will be better than another in improving their lives or delivering the benefits they seek. It can often motivate them to take immediate action, like trying a new brand, redeeming a coupon or requesting more information.

- **Reassurance:**

Before a buyer completes her purchase, advertising can help her confirm that she is getting what she wants. Even after the transaction has been made, advertising plays a role by reminding a consumer why she spent her money and reassuring her that she made the right choice.

- **Simplifying Shopping:**

By reducing a consumer's need to search for products or the stores that stock them, advertising makes shopping simpler and more time-efficient. It helps eliminate unnecessary risk-taking and facilitates easier decision-making at the point of purchase.

- **Moderating Prices:**

In many product categories, like airlines and cars, advertising stimulates direct price competition. More generally, it reduces marketing and distribution expenses over time by keeping people informed, motivating them to buy, and encouraging high-volume and repeat purchases. Also, because a single advertisement can simultaneously influence millions of consumers, it is more cost-efficient than personal selling and other customized marketing tools. Over time, these cost reductions help firms hold down the prices they charge consumers.

DRASTIC CHANGE IN TODAY'S ADVERTISEMENT

In honour of Pandora's 10th anniversary, the senior vice president of ad product and strategy shares the top 10 major changes in advertising that have occurred during the last decade.

1. Mobile Mania:

In 2007, Steve Jobs delivered his most iconic device: the iPhone. Like the Internet before it, the iPhone revolutionized the way consumers connected, consumed, and exchanged information.

Advertising changed along with it, as marketers became responsible for driving mobile revenue. Audio ads proved a perfect fit for mobile because they allowed brands to reach people regardless of screen size or location. The mobile world continues to grow faster than anyone could have forecasted. Statistics show that mobile ad spending is expected to top $28 billion this year.

2. Data-Driven:

In today's "show me you know me" culture, people share all kinds of information about themselves. This shows that consumers have changed the way they think about brands having data on them. They expect brands to make their lives better because advertisers can know more about them. When consumers enable publisher access to their behaviour, it's assumed that all following experiences with ads and content are specifically curated just for them.

3. Quality Matters:

Publishers and ad tech companies are becoming even more accountable for the inventory they sell, and have to invest in more transparency measures. Marketers need to be open to paying more for real people and real attention, but this does pay off in the end.

4. Bite-Sized Content:

As people consume content on the fly, the content is getting smaller and smaller. It also needs to be delivered incredibly quickly. The message to advertisers is clear: get the immediate attention of consumers, or they will be off to the next thing.

5. Multi-Layered Media: The Attention Economy is Here:

People used to consume one form of media at a time, but now they have many apps running at once. They're watching TV, while simultaneously on posting on Twitter, viewing their Instagram feed, and shopping on Amazon. Consumer attention is at a premium, as this fragmentation makes it difficult for marketers to earn it.

6. Internet of Things:

No longer on only a computer, a television, or a phone, people are consuming content where they want and on whatever device they desire. Now it's wearable, in your car, or even on your fridge. Wherever the content goes, the advertising must follow. As this trend continues, I predict that audio ads will become more important than ever.

7. Keep it Simple:

We first saw this with Google's bare-bones homepage, followed by the debut of Amazon's one-click ordering. Marketers have heard the message loud and clear: simple services win. If consumers can't do it in three clicks or less, they're not sticking around.

8. Connected Kids with Real Money:

Powerful, pocket-sized technology has transformed kids into young consumers faster than any generation before. Nearly all teens – 92 percent – go online every day and one-fourth is online "constantly," according to the Pew Research Center. They're not just interacting with friends; they're shopping, too. And frictionless mobile payment integrations will only give these kids more spending power in the future.

9. Offline ROI in Fewer Than Three Clicks:

Someone can see a Domino's ad, click three times, and eat a pizza without ever having to speak to anyone. People expect to buy what they want when they want it. Famed Internet analyst Mary

Meeker points out that buy buttons optimized for mobile users have popped up on Twitter, Facebook, and Google, amongst other interesting trends.

10. Consumers are the New Spokespeople:

The rise of social media has caused advertisers to lean more on consumers as the faces of their brands. The consumers bring authenticity as the people who use the products, and other consumers trust them. Your friend the "crafty mom," "lazy mom," "hip mom," or "working mom," plus their Instagram followers, is the new media buy.

Devices plus connectivity will continue to accelerate and power the transformation of media and the practice of advertising to consumers. To survive and prosper in this hyper-competitive, fast-moving world, brands must be agile, and able to adapt and react quickly.